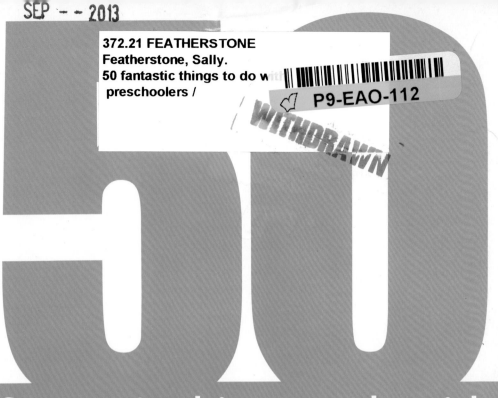

50

fantastic things to do with
Preschoolers

SALLY AND PHILL FEATHERSTONE

BULK PURCHASE

Gryphon House books are available for special premiums and sales promotions as well as for fund-raising use. Special editions or book excerpts also can be created to specification. For details, contact the Director of Marketing at Gryphon House.

DISCLAIMER

Gryphon House, Inc. and the authors cannot be held responsible for damage, mishap, or injury incurred during the use of or because of activities in this book. Appropriate and reasonable caution and adult supervision of children involved in activities and corresponding to the age and capability of each child involved is recommended at all times. Do not leave children unattended at any time. Observe safety and caution at all times.

GH10048 | A Gryphon House Book

Parenting

50 Fantastic Things to Do With Preschoolers

Gryphon
House, Inc.
Lewisville, NC

SALLY AND PHILL FEATHERSTONE

50 FANTASTIC THINGS TO DO WITH PRESCHOOLERS

by Sally and Phill Featherstone

COPYRIGHT

© 2013 Gryphon House, Inc.
Published by Gryphon House, Inc.
P.O. Box 10, Lewisville, NC 27023
800.638.0928 (phone); 877.638.7576 (fax)

Visit us on the web at www.gryphonhouse.com
Originally published in 2010 by A&C Black Publishers Limited.

LIBRARY OF CONGRESS CATALOGING-IN-PUBLICATION DATA

Featherstone, Sally.
  50 fantastic things to do with preschoolers / by Sally and Phill Featherstone.
     pages cm
  Includes index.
   ISBN 978-0-87659-467-4
  1. Child development. 2. Education, Preschool--Activity programs. 3. Education, Preschool--Parent participation. 4. Children's plays. I. Featherstone, Phill. II. Title.
   HQ772.F3793 2013
   372.21--dc23
                        2012044471

Contents

Introduction

There's plenty of research to show that babies and children who enjoy a stimulating home environment learn better and more quickly. So what parents and caregivers do to lay the groundwork for learning early on is an investment that pays back throughout their child's life.

This book has been specially written for parents to use with their young children at home. However, it can also be used by caregivers and workers in daycare and childcare settings. It contains 50 simple activities that can be done easily with very little equipment, often in your spare time. It's not a course to work through. All the ideas here are suitable for children from 36–50 months, and in many cases beyond. Choose what you and your child enjoy, as one of the main aims of this book is fun!

There are few things as delightful or rewarding as being alongside young children as they explore, inquire, experiment, and learn. Join your child in her enthusiasm for learning!

There are three books in the 50 Fantastic Things series:

50 Fantastic Things to Do with Babies (suitable for use from soon after birth to 20 months)
50 Fantastic Things to Do with Toddlers (suitable for use from 16–36 months)
50 Fantastic Things to Do with Preschoolers (suitable for use from 36–50 months)

The age groupings above are approximate and are only suggestions. Children develop at different speeds. They also grow in spurts, with some periods of rapid development alternating with other times when they don't seem to change as quickly. So don't worry if your child doesn't seem ready for a particular activity. Try another instead and return to it later. On the other hand, if your child gets on well and quickly, try some of the ideas in the "Another idea" and "Ready for more?" sections.

A NOTE ON SAFETY

Care must be taken at all times when dealing with babies and young children. Common sense will be your main guide, but here are a few ideas to help you have fun safely.

Babies and young children naturally explore things by bringing them to their mouths. This is fine, but always check that toys and other objects you use are clean.

Although rare, swallowing objects or choking on them is a hazard. Some children are more susceptible than others. If you are concerned about choking, buy a choking tester from a retail baby supply store.

Baby's lungs are delicate. They need clean air. Never smoke near your child, and don't allow anyone else to do so.

Children are naturally inquisitive, and you will want to encourage this. However, secure and happy children are often unaware of danger. Your baby needs you to watch out for her. Make sure you are always there. You can't watch your baby all the time, but don't leave her alone and unsupervised for more than a few minutes at a time. Even when she is asleep, check on her regularly.

The objects and toys we suggest here have been chosen for their safety. Nevertheless, most things can be dangerous if they go wrong or are not used properly:

- Mobiles and toys tied to baby gyms are great to encourage looking and reaching, but check that they are fastened securely.
- Ribbons and string are fascinating to children, but they can be a choking hazard. They can also become wrapped around arms, legs, and necks.
- Children are natural explorers. They need clean floors. Store outdoor shoes away from areas where your child will be playing.
- Take care with furniture, and look out for trip hazards. Pad sharp edges of tables and other furniture

HELPFUL HINTS

Some children find it difficult to remember things in abstract. Your child might find it easier to play this game in the bedroom or bathroom.

Bedtime Teddy!
practicing routines

WHAT YOU NEED:

- a teddy or doll with removable clothes
- a onesie or pajamas for the teddy bear (desirable, but not essential)
- baby toothbrush
- washcloth
- a doll's bed or a box for a bed
- some fabric for bedclothes—an old pillowcase and a fleece would be good as they don't fray

Ready for more?

Make this game a regular feature of bedtime, so your child begins to have a sense of responsibility for her toy.

WHAT TO DO:

1. Make the bed ready for the toy. Let your child put the pillow and sheets on and cover it with the fleece.
2. Now ask your child to tell you what the toy needs to do before it goes to bed. Help her think by talking about what she does before she goes to bed.
3. Find some of the things your child talks about: a toothbrush and toothpaste, a washcloth, a comb, a storybook, or a tiny teddy bear for the toy. Now help get the toy ready for bed, talking with your child as she prepares the toy.
4. When the toy is safely tucked in bed, you could read a story and cuddle with it.
5. Now help your child be a parent by clearing up and putting away all the things you used, tiptoeing around so as not to wake the teddy bear or doll. Then you could cuddle, too!

Another idea: If the teddy bear or doll is waterproof, you could give it a bath before you put it to bed. Or you could give it a pretend bath in an empty bowl.

Mine and Yours
naming and recognizing objects

WHAT YOU NEED:

Some pairs of objects—one of yours and one belonging to your child, such as:

- your hat and his hat
- your shoe and his shoe
- your hairbrush and his hairbrush
- your sock and his sock

Ready for more?

Add some baby or doll clothes to the game and sort three ways, asking, "Who does this belong to?" Let your child fetch the doll or teddy to join the game.

WHAT TO DO:

1. Sit with your child, and look at all the things you have collected.
2. Now, take a pair of objects.
3. Hold both objects out to your child and, using his name, ask (for example), "Which is Evan's hat? Which hat is yours?"
4. Encourage him to look carefully and choose the object that is his own.
5. Praise his efforts and say, "Yes, that's your hat. This is my hat." Play again.

Another idea: Encourage your child to sort the objects and clothing into two piles.

DID YOU KNOW?

It takes many children a while to recognize themselves as a separate person.

HELPFUL HINTS

If your child finds it difficult to recognize his own belongings, remind him each time he gets dressed by saying, "This is your coat, isn't it, Matt? We are putting on Matt's coat." Put a coat hook low down in your hall, so your child can begin to find and look after his own belongings.

What is your child learning?

This game will help your child realize he is a separate person and that he has belongings. This is a great step in learning to be independent.

Stomp and Clap
wrist bells

WHAT YOU NEED:

- some baby wrist toys— bells and rattles

Ready for more?

Put the wristbands on and dance to the radio or a favorite CD.

What is your child learning?

Your child is learning how to coordinate her hands and feet. This will help her strengthen the muscles in these areas of her body.

WHAT TO DO:

1. If you haven't got any wrist toys, find some bracelets or bangles for your child to wear. Several of these will make a good sound.

2. Keep the wrist toys out of sight till you have practiced this little song. You could sing it to the tune of "Frère Jacques":

I am clapping, I am clapping
Here I come, here I come
Can you see me clapping?
Can you hear me clapping?
Here I come, here I come.

3. You can change the words to add stomping, shaking, or waving for more verses.

4. Now bring the wrist toys where your child can see them, and offer her some to wear on her wrists or ankles. You could wear some, too.

5. Sing the song again and clap your hands as you sing.

Another idea: Collect a basket of gloves and play the same game with these.

DID YOU KNOW?

Clapping along to music is good for body control.

HELPFUL HINTS

If your child finds it difficult to listen and move at the same time, play the game sitting on the sofa or the floor.

If your child is reluctant to join in, start with a doll or stuffed animal. Make sure that your child's feet are thoroughly washed and dried when you've finished.

What is your child learning?

Feeling the different textures and talking about what they are and how they feel will help language development. Discussing the properties of what is in the trays increases knowledge and understanding of the world.

Bare Feet
textures and feet

DID YOU KNOW?

Feeling different textures stimulates the sensory receptors in the brain.

WHAT YOU NEED:

- four plastic trays, tubs or box lids (they don't all have to be the same size or shape)
- warm, soapy water and a towel
- cold, wet sand
- tiny pebbles or gravel
- fur fabric or a small blanket

Ready for more?

Try making footprints on black paper with water. Put some paint on a tray or tin lid and draw with your feet.

WHAT TO DO:

1. Put some warm, soapy water in one tray or tub. In the second, put a layer of cold, damp sand. Put some pebbles in the third. Cover the base of the fourth with the fur fabric or blanket.
2. Take off yours and your child's shoes and socks. Play a game of Copy Me, wiggling your toes, pointing them in the air, walking on your heels, and so on.
3. Feel the coldness of the kitchen floor, the texture of the living room carpet, and so on.
4. Take turns to step into and out of each tray. Start with the sand and finish with the water. Don't rush it, and talk about what you are doing and how it feels.
5. Work your way through the trays and finish with a dip in clean, warm water, tickling your child's toes as you dry them.

Fingers and Thumbs
fingerpainting

WHAT YOU NEED:

- big sheets of paper
- aprons
- a washable surface
- some fingerpaints—you can make these at home
- a bowl of warm water and a towel

Ready for more?

Give your child a toy car to run through the paint, making tracks through the paint and onto the paper. Make handprints by putting your hands in the saucers and printing them on paper or cardboard. Talk about the differences between your hands and hers.

WHAT TO DO:

1. Put your aprons on.
2. If you want to make your own fingerpaint, help your child to mix a few tablespoons of cornstarch or flour with some water. Add some food coloring. Put each color in a separate saucer.
3. Put the paper on a flat surface on a table or the floor.
4. Put the bowls or pots of paint in the middle of the table and show your child how to scoop some of the paint onto the paper. Move the paint around with your fingers and the palms of your hands. Use both hands and show her that you are enjoying it!
5. Now let your child explore the paint with her fingers and hands.
6. Don't worry if your child makes a mess—painting is messy!
7. As soon as she has had enough, let her wash her hands in warm, bubbly water.

What is your child learning?

Your child is learning about the texture of things and how they behave when she pushes and pokes them.

DID YOU KNOW?

Manipulating and feeling messy and tactile materials helps strengthen hand muscles.

DID YOU KNOW?

Wrist, hand, and finger muscles are all important for drawing and writing. Start young!

Pat-a-Cake
making pastry

WHAT YOU NEED:

- flour
- water in a small bottle or jug
- a bowl
- a spoon
- a board, table, or worktop space
- aprons

WHAT TO DO:

1. Put on your aprons.
2. Help your child to spoon six tablespoons of flour into the bowl and pour a little water on it.
3. Your child can mix the flour and water to make a thick dough, adding more water if it's too thick and more flour if it's too sticky.
4. When the dough sticks together, help your child lift it out onto the board or surface.
5. Now, make some dough for yourself.
6. Pat and poke the dough together with fingers and hands.
7. Sing the "Pat-a-Cake" song:

   Pat-a-cake, pat-a-cake, baker's man
   Bake me a cake as fast as you can
   Roll it and pat it and mark it with B
   And put it in the oven for Baby and me.

8. Change the letter and name to the name of your child.

Another idea: You could bake the pastry, but it doesn't taste very nice!

What is your child learning?

To begin with, your child may simply spray in all directions! However, let her have several tries over a number of days, and she will probably start to think about what she is doing and will compose the colors.

Color Spray
using spray bottles

WHAT YOU NEED:

- some spray bottles (get ones that are easy to squeeze and check that the trigger isn't too far away for small hands to grip)
- thin paint or food coloring mixed with water (red, blue, and green should be enough)
- paper or fabric

WHAT TO DO:

You need a fine day for this activity. The aim is to make a picture using a spray and colors.

1. Pin or tape a sheet of paper or fabric to a fence or outside door.
2. Fill the spray bottles with the colors (thin paint or food coloring plus water).
3. Encourage your child to experiment with the sprays. You may need to show her how to work the spray bottle first, but don't take over the painting!
4. You might want to distract your child with something else while the first round of paint dries, and then continue later.
5. When your child's masterpiece is dry, don't throw it away—use it. You can pin it up in her bedroom, use it for wrapping paper, or paste it to the lid of her toy box.

DID YOU KNOW?

Some children don't achieve 20/20 vision until they are about two years old.

Ready for more?

Paint a simple picture on a smooth surface and encourage your child to use a water spray to wash it off. Use a spray bottle to water plants or wash windows.

Another idea: Use a spray bottle with clean water to wash outdoor toys.

What is your child learning?

This activity is good for physical development and for encouraging exploration and spatial awareness. Developing the story will stimulate creativity.

Through the Tunnel
enjoying play tunnels and tents

WHAT YOU NEED:

- a play tunnel or pop-up play tent (if you don't have one, you can make one by draping a sheet or blanket over a couple of dining chairs or a clothes rack)

WHAT TO DO:

1. Involve your child in the preparations. Let him watch and encourage him to help you erect the tent or tunnel. If you are making it yourself, use plenty of tape and/or pegs to fix the sheet securely to the chairs or rack.
2. Sit at one end of the tunnel. Encourage your child to crawl through it to you. It's helpful if you can do this with another adult, so your child can crawl between you. If not, getting him to crawl toward his favorite stuffed animal should get him started.
3. Praise your child when he gets to the end of the tunnel.
4. Be a fun monster and chase your child into the tunnel. Don't get serious—keep it light-hearted.

Ready for more?

Make up a simple story about a monster, your child, and the tunnel or cave. Role-play the story.

Another idea: Reverse the roles—have your child chase you!

Stickers and Stars
fun with fingers

WHAT YOU NEED:

- some washable felt-tipped pens
- some small, self-adhesive labels
- a selection of star stickers (different colors if possible)

Ready for more?

Make a collection of rings, bracelets, and necklaces (or make some yourself out of colored yarn). Play at putting these on each other and on stuffed animals.

WHAT TO DO:

1. Put a star sticker on both of your child's index fingers and on your own.
2. Hold your index fingers in the air. Wave the stars about. Start with the stars high up, reaching as high as you can, and swoosh them down like shooting stars. Encourage your child to join in. Shake your fingers to make the stars "twinkle."
3. Now put a star sticker on every one of your child's fingers and on all of yours. Sing "Twinkle, Twinkle, Little Star."

Another idea: Draw bird shapes on stickers and stick them on your hands. Sing the "Two Little Dickie Birds" rhyme and do the actions.

DID YOU KNOW?

Finger play is important for developing brain connections.

HELPFUL HINTS

Take it slowly, particularly when you start. It may take your child time to register what's going on before she joins in. Lots of repetition helps. Reflective, fluorescent stickers will help catch your child's attention and make the game more visually stimulating.

What is your child learning?

This activity helps development in a lot of areas—fine movement and control, language, linking words with actions, copying and imitating.

Transparent Colors
a color-changing treasure basket

WHAT YOU NEED:

- a basket full of multi-colored objects (such as transparent colored paper and shapes, colored fabrics and netting, or kaleidoscopes or viewers)
- a white blanket, sheet, or rug

WHAT TO DO:

1. Spread out the sheet, rug, or blanket on the floor. Place the basket of transparent colored objects on it.

2. Together, explore the contents of the basket. Pick them up one by one and look at them. Take turns to peer through the kaleidoscopes and viewers. Talk about them—their colors, how they make things look, and how they feel.

3. Try layering one of the transparent objects over another. How does this alter the colors? Move one over the other and look at how the colors change.

4. Ask your child simple questions, and encourage him to repeat some of the words you are using to describe the objects and how you are playing with them.

DID YOU
KNOW?

Some children are natural "snackers" and may need a very small meal every hour!

Veggies and Dips
snack-time choices

WHAT YOU NEED:

- vegetables to cut into "dippers"—carrots, celery, peppers, cucumber
- little breadsticks
- plain yogurt
- tomato ketchup
- chopped chives

WHAT TO DO:

This activity is about making healthy choices.

1. Let your child watch or help as you divide the yogurt into some little bowls. Leave one bowl plain, and make some flavored dips with the rest.

2. Now cut the vegetables into sticks and arrange these on a plate. Use vegetables that your child likes, with perhaps one new one. Put out some breadsticks or a few crackers, too.

3. Now sit with your child for a snack. Remember that she will be influenced by your behavior and your choices, so make good choices yourself! Talk about what you choose and encourage her to try foods.

4. The important thing is to get your child to try new foods, so if she tries something and doesn't like it, don't force her to eat it.

Another idea: Have choices of vegetables with meals whenever you can. Let your child help herself—she will have a good idea of how much she can eat. Be sure to praise her for trying new things.

My Baby
baby-doll play

DID YOU KNOW?

All children need a secure, safe, loving environment for their brains to thrive.

WHAT YOU NEED:

- a baby doll
- baby clothes, diapers, bottle, pacifier
- a cot, blankets, or stroller

Ready for more?

Play with toy baby animals and toy people. Talk about how animals and people look after babies and keep them safe. Look at mother-and-baby books, as well as books about baby animals. Look out for DVDs and television programs to watch. Talk together about the book or DVD.

WHAT TO DO:

This activity isn't just for girls. It's important for males to develop caring and nurturing skills, too. Besides, most boys will enjoy playing with dolls at this age.

1. Sit down with your child, the baby doll, and the various items you've gathered. Talk about them and what they are all for with your child.

2. Talk to the doll, and talk to your child about the doll. Give the doll a name. Take turns to cuddle and stroke the baby. (If you have two dolls, sometimes it works better to have one each; but if not, you can still talk and play together.)

3. Start to role-play being a parent. The baby is sleepy. Rock the doll gently and sing a nursery rhyme. When the "baby" is asleep (let your child decide when this is), lay it down and cover it up.

4. Talk about your baby being tired, hungry, or needing to be changed. Go through the play of meeting these needs—feeding, changing, and putting to bed. At each stage, talk about how the baby feels. Encourage your child to contribute words and ideas.

Another idea: Young children are usually fascinated by babies. If there's a baby among your friends or family, try to let your child spend some time with him.

Some baby dolls are quite large. Make sure you have one that is small enough for your child to handle comfortably. Learn some new baby songs. There are lots of Internet sites that have them, some with tunes as well as lyrics. Put "lullaby songs" in your search engine.

What is your child learning?

Learning to care and demonstrating care and love are important as your child moves beyond an exclusive focus on himself and toward becoming aware of the needs and feelings of others.

Just like Me
an action game

WHAT YOU NEED:

- a selection of stuffed animals

Ready for more?

Let your child take the lead, choosing the actions. Follow her, and encourage her to talk about what she is doing. Play a "follow me" game around the house, going into and out of rooms, walking in silly ways, and making gestures.

What is your child learning?

Imitating and copying are among the main techniques your child has for learning. Watching you closely and following what you do will also develop her observational skills.

WHAT TO DO:

1. Start by sitting down with your child. Tell her that you want her to do everything you do.
2. Wave your arms in the air and sing, "Wave your arms, wave your arms, just like me." Encourage your child to copy you. Reward her with praise and smiles when she does.
3. When your child has got the hang of this, sing, "Shake your head, shake your head, just like me," and encourage copying. Continue with "waggle your hands," "rub your chest," "pat your knees," and so on.
4. Take a stuffed animal and encourage your child to do the same. Move the toy and sing, getting your child to shadow the toy's movements and join in. For example: "Look at teddy jumping, look at teddy jumping, way up high."

Another idea: Repeat an action you've done before but with a minor change. Encourage your child to watch closely and copy you exactly.

HELPFUL HINTS

If your child needs help starting, begin with toys that make a noise. When you each have one, make the noise and encourage her to copy you. Lots of repetition will help her get the most out of this activity, so don't move on from one stage to another too soon.

Everything in Its Place
cleaning up

WHAT YOU NEED:

- a basket of items belonging to your child, collected from around your home

WHAT TO DO:

Use this game to help your child learn the proper places for things, and have fun putting them away!

1. Tip the objects out of the basket onto the floor.
2. Pick one up. See if your child can name it. Ask if he can tell you where it belongs. Be prepared to give him clues if he doesn't know.
3. Once you've established where the item goes, ask your child to take it there. You may need to go with him to help with doors, drawers, and lids. Once he has put the item away successfully, give him lots of praise. Then, ask your child to choose another item and repeat until he is tired of the game.

Another idea: Play a reverse version of the game. Give your child the name of an object and ask him to find it and bring it to the basket.

What is your child learning?

Tidying up for your child will not teach him, and it will irritate you. Learning that objects have clear places to go is an important organizational skill. This activity, with plenty of fun and rewards, will help your child learn the importance of organizing and looking after his own possessions.

Ready for more?

It may take your child some time to get the hang of this and be able to tell you where things go. Help him think and work it out, but if he can't do this, help by taking him to the place and showing him. Have a "cleaning-up basket." Encourage your child to use it to put his toys away.

Snip Snap
early cutting

WHAT YOU NEED:

- child's safety scissors
- plenty of scrap paper (junk mail, old magazines, wrapping paper, envelopes)

Ready for more?

Fringe the edges of a drawing or painting. Make a pattern by cutting colored and shiny paper into strips and sticking them on cardboard. For a change, let your child hold the paper while you snip.

WHAT TO DO:

This activity is about self-assurance and confidence in the use of a tool for cutting. It's not about accurate cutting out.

1. Cut some of the paper into long thin strips. Your child needs to be able to snip across the strips in one cut.
2. Leave some of the paper in larger pieces.
3. Sit down with your child. Show her how to hold and use the scissors. Be sensitive to hand preference by getting her to try both hands and settling on the one she finds most natural. Talk about cutting and snipping.
4. Encourage your child to cut the papers, snipping the long strips into bits and snipping round the edges of the larger pieces.
5. Give her help if she needs it by holding the paper as she snips or by putting your hand over hers on the scissors.

Another idea: Work together to make some place mats by snipping the edges of squares of colored paper in a fringe.

What is your child learning?

Using scissors is a good example of simple tool operation. It requires higher levels of coordination of eye-hand. Lots of practice will develop facility in handling scissors and tools, too.

You can get special scissors for left handers, but many young children are still experimenting with both hands, so be sure that your child really is left handed before buying these.

Rocking Teddy
a rocking snuggle song

WHAT YOU NEED:

- a blanket or piece of soft fabric—stretchy fabric works best
- a cushion
- a favorite stuffed animal or teddy bear

WHAT TO DO:

1. Put the cushion on the floor and sit your child on it.
2. Sit down opposite. Give your child the stuffed animal and wrap the blanket gently around his shoulders.
3. Grip the blanket firmly at the edges and rock gently from side to side.
4. As you rock gently with your child opposite you, rocking in the blanket, sing:

Rocking softly, rocking slow
Gently, gently, here we go.
Hugging Teddy, keeping warm
Keeping safe and out of harm.

The tune to "Twinkle, Twinkle, Little Star" works well, or you can make up your own.

Ready for more?

Use a blanket to make a small hammock for stuffed animals. Rock them gently, singing this song or "Rock-a-Bye, Baby." When you have played the game, hang the hammock above your child's bed, cot, or changing mat.

What is your child learning?

Feeling safe, secure, and valued helps the development of self-confidence and self-assurance. It also encourages feelings of trust.

HELPFUL HINTS

This is a good activity to do with very active children and works well after a bath and before bed. It will help your child feel safe, secure, and probably sleepy.

DID YOU KNOW?

Using both hands stimulates both sides of the brain.

Five Little Peas
popping and placing

WHAT YOU NEED:

- some peas in their shells
- small bowls

Ready for more?

Say this rhyme. You need to make a fist and open your fingers one at a time as the pod pops: "Five fat peas in a pea pod pressed/ one grew, two grew, so did all the rest/ They grew and grew and did not stop/ till one fine day when the pod went POP!"

WHAT TO DO:

1. Wash the pea pods before you and your child play with them.
2. Sit in the kitchen with your child, and look at the pea pods and any leaves or tendrils that are attached to them. Talk about the pea pods growing on a plant in a farmer's field.
3. Show your child how to press her thumb on the end of the pod (not the stalk end) so it pops open. Listen for the little pop!
4. Now show her how to open the pod carefully so she can see the peas all in a row. Count them together. Let her take the peas out of the pod and put them in a bowl.
5. Look at the inside of the pea pod and how it is shaped to fit the peas.

What is your child learning?

This activity will help with concentration and perseverance. Your child will also be learning the crucial actions of bringing her finger and thumb together in a pincer movement.

Let's Eat
making a simple snack

WHAT YOU NEED:

- bread
- a toaster or grill
- butter or margarine
- blunt knives (little butter knives or plastic picnic knives are ideal)
- something to spread on top—jam, honey, cheese spread, and so on

WHAT TO DO:

1. Get all the items together. Make sure the butter is taken out of the fridge in early enough so it's not too hard to spread.
2. Tell your child you're going to make a snack.
3. Make some toast. Stress the importance of keeping away from hot things, but let your child be involved by watching you.
4. Cut the toast into half or quarter slices.
5. Talk to him about the spreads you have available, and choose one for him to spread. Encourage him to ask you for what he wants, using *please* and *thank you* as you pass things to each other and wait for answers.
6. Give your child help spreading if he needs it, but the more he can do for himself, the better.

Another idea: Go shopping with your child for the ingredients for his snack.

Ready for more?

Plan a picnic. Involve your child in choosing, gathering and packing the food. Let your child make his own lunch or after-care snack. Try making something more ambitious than toast: beans on toast or even a simple pizza.

What is your child learning?

Independent activities that involve negotiation and choice encourage brain growth. Making a choice also develops the concept of action and consequence.

HELPFUL HINTS

Too many choices can bewilder some children. Limit what you offer him in the beginning. Give attention to using the correct words for things and to using the knife properly for spreading.

DID YOU KNOW?

Learning to make and communicate a choice is an important stage in brain development.

Making Faces
a book of expressions

WHAT YOU NEED:

- a collection of magazine pages with people's faces showing a range of expressions (newspaper color supplements and celebrity magazines are good sources)

Ready for more?

Play How Do I Feel? Make a face and ask your child to say what you are feeling. This makes a fun family game.

What is your child learning?

Learning to "read" and empathize with another person's feelings is a key human skill. This activity will help your child to begin to think about and respond to how other people feel.

WHAT TO DO:

This activity is quite sophisticated and therefore suitable for children who are older. If your child doesn't seem to get it, put it aside and try again in a few weeks.

1. Sit in a comfortable chair with your child and look at one of the magazines. When you come to a picture of a face, ask your child how she thinks that person is feeling.
2. Find a photo of someone smiling. Look carefully at his mouth and eyes. Ask your child if she can make a smiling face. Praise her when she gets it right.
3. Now say, "Can you make your face sad (or grumpy or scared or disappointed)?" Keep looking at the pictures and practice different expressions together.
4. Talk about how you feel when you're happy, mad, sorry, or sad.
5. Talk about how you know what other people are feeling. "How do you know when Mommy's mad?" or, "How do you know when (friend's name)'s upset?"

Another idea: When you read stories to your child, talk about how the people in the story are feeling.

HELPFUL HINTS

For an easier start, pick out a few extreme expressions—such as somebody laughing or crying—and talk about those first. Use a mirror so you child can see her expressions and practice them.

DID YOU KNOW?

When we say that someone can't relate to other people, it may just be lack of experience.

Fetch It for Me
under a blanket

YOU NEED:

- a big sheet of fabric, such as an old sheet or curtain
- a basket of objects to hide—stuffed animals, cars, balls

Ready for more?

Play Chase the Feet. Take off your shoes and put your legs under the sheet. Move them around and let your child see if he can catch them through the sheet.

WHAT TO DO:

1. Spread the sheet on the carpet or the grass.
2. Sit at the edge with your child, lift the sheet, and peep underneath.
3. Lift the edge up and put it over your heads so you can see under the sheet. Can you see to the other side?
4. Now take a stuffed animal, fold the sheet back, put the toy down and pull the sheet over it. For the first time, put the toy quite near the edge to build confidence.
5. Ask your child, "Can you see where your teddy bear is? Can you go under the sheet and fetch him?" If your child is hesitant, go under together and fetch the toy.
6. Play again with a different toy. Praise him for being brave.

Another idea: Let your child go under the sheet and hide a toy for you to fetch. Help him by holding the edge of the sheet to help him.

HELPFUL HINTS

Use a small blanket to play Guess What? Put some toys under the blanket and see if your child can guess what they are by feeling through the blanket or by putting his hands under it. Some children are really frightened by this sort of game. Stay with him, and make sure the sheet is small enough for him to stand up and get out when he wants to.

What is your child learning?

This game will build your child's confidence. He is learning that you are a constant feature of his life and that you will keep him safe.

My Bath Crayons
mark making

WHAT YOU NEED:

- a pack of bath crayons
- a flat plastic lid for each of you (from plastic boxes)
- nail brushes, old toothbrushes, and sponges
- warm soapy water and a towel
- aprons or old clothes

Ready for more?

Let your child help with the dishes by offering a dish cloth to clean child-friendly utensils, plastic plates, and so on.

What is your child learning?

Your child is learning that she can make her own marks with no fear of being "right" or "wrong." This is very important in building a can-do attitude.

WHAT TO DO:

1. Put a bit of water on the lids to make them damp.
2. Now experiment with the bath crayons, making marks, circles, and wiggly lines. Talk about what you are doing—this will keep your child focused.
3. Keep showing each other what you have done, and give your child praise for her effort and the different sorts of marks she makes.
4. When you have plenty of bath crayon markings on your lids, use nail brushes, old toothbrushes, or sponges to move the color around the lid and make patterns in the colors.
5. When you have finished, help your child wash the lids and her hands in warm soapy water and dry them carefully.

Another idea: Take long pieces of string outside and trail them through puddles or bowls of water, and then trail them along the sidewalk or patio.

DID YOU KNOW?

Activities like this will stimulate the whole brain!

Can You Find?
animal sounds

WHAT YOU NEED:

- some toy farm animals—familiar ones such as a cow, a pig, a sheep, a chicken, a horse, a cat, or a dog

WHAT TO DO:

1. Start the game by playing with the animals and making their noises. Walk them across the carpet toward each other, making the sounds.
2. Now say, "I'm going to ask you a question. Are you ready?"
3. When your child is ready, say "Can you find the animal that says 'Moo'?" When your child fetches the animal, reward him with praise and smiles.
4. Continue to play with the different animals, making the sounds for your child as clues.
5. If he wants to ask you a question, let him.
6. When your child has had enough, play a different game with the animals, or leave him for free play.

Ready for more?

Make a scrapbook of animals, cutting the pictures from magazines or using clip art from the Internet. If your child has a favorite animal, make him a photo book of cats, dogs, elephants—whatever he chooses.

HELPFUL HINTS

Every time you play a new game, go slowly in the beginning. Watch your child play for a while, and play the same game again after a few days so he gets used to it. Just use two or three animals when you start the game, and reduce distractions by switching off the television or radio.

What is your child learning?

Talking and playing games lets your child know that you are interested in him. This is an important thing for children to learn. Confident children who feel secure and valued make better progress.

Encourage reluctant children to get involved by modeling the fun yourself. If you find messy play difficult, try not to show it! Your model is essential for your child's all-around development. Some children find it difficult to point just one finger. Help your child gently, but don't force it. The movement will come in time.

What is your child learning?

Your child is learning skills that will prepare her hands and fingers, as well as her brain, for the important tasks of reading and writing.

Texture Play
mark making in shaving cream

WHAT YOU NEED:

- some shaving cream in an aerosol can (un-perfumed and non-allergenic
- pieces of cardboard, scissors
- old loyalty or credit cards, sticks, and sponges
- a flat, washable surface, such as a tabletop

Ready for more?

Try using fingerpaint or foam on the tiles by the bath for some easy-to-wash-off fun together at bath time.

WHAT TO DO:

1. Sit with your child and talk about shaving cream, looking at the can together.
2. Now, spray some shaving cream on the flat surface and let your child explore it with her hands and fingers.
3. Join in and play with her, using your fingers to make marks in the foam. Encourage your child to make circles, swirls, zigzags ,or even letters—but keep it free and fun.
4. Cut some pieces of cardboard about 3 inches long. Cut zigzags and other shapes in the edge of each piece to make patterned scrapers.
5. Now, try making marks with either the scrapers you have made or old credit or loyalty cards.

Another idea: Add some paint or food coloring to the foam.

DID YOU **KNOW?**
Mark making in messy play helps children's brains get used to recognizing patterns.

Snap, Crackle, Pop
making sounds with feet and hands

WHAT YOU NEED:

A range of materials that make sounds:

- bubble wrap
- tissue paper
- chocolate box or other food liners
- foil
- empty chip bags

WHAT TO DO:

1. Put all the materials you have collected on the floor.
2. Sit with your child and look at all the things. Experiment with scrunching, popping, and feeling with your fingers.
3. Now take off your shoes and socks, and stand up to explore the materials with your feet. Stamp, hop, and jump, popping the bubble wrap, crunching the tissue, flattening the chocolate box liners and chip bags.
4. Talk about how they feel: *crinkly, poppy, crunchy, smooth*—and how they sound—like fireworks, like raindrops.

Another idea: Collect some smooth, fluffy, and soft materials and objects for a different sort of feeling.

Ready for more?

Try painting on bubble wrap or foil using paint with a little white glue added.

Take your shoes and socks off and walk around your house, feeling all the different surfaces and textures with your feet and toes.

HELPFUL HINTS

Hold your child's hands if he is still a bit wobbly on uneven surfaces. This activity is very good for balance and confidence. Some children don't like being barefoot. If this is the case with your child, make sure the room is warm and comfortable, and just have bare feet for a short time.

What is your child learning?

In exploring textures and objects with hands and feet, your child is finding out about the world.

What is your child learning?

Learning about tools such as pens and other mark makers is the first stage in learning to draw, write, dig, eat, hammer, and so on. This activity gives your child practice and an adult model to follow.

A Basket of Markers
exploring colors

DID YOU KNOW?

Children get a great sense of security from clear rules, but don't have too many!

WHAT YOU NEED:

- a big piece of paper and painter's tape, which peels off without damaging surfaces
- some children's big felt pens or crayons
- a flat vertical space—the back of a door, the front of a big fridge, a big piece of cardboard from a packing box

Ready for more?

Find a place in your house where you can display your child's mark making and first "pictures."

WHAT TO DO:

1. Stick the paper on the flat surface—make it reach down to the floor and up to the highest point your child can reach. Put the basket of crayons or markers on the floor by the paper.
2. Sit or kneel with your child in front of the paper, and encourage her to start making marks. Remember that mark making is a first stage and comes before drawing objects or people.
3. Join in and talk together about what you are doing. Use simple color words as you work, and describe the marks—"I'm doing some wiggly lines up here at the top," or "I'm going to use red now."
4. Continue to draw until your child has had enough, or leave the drawing so she can come back and add more marks later.

HELPFUL HINTS

Short sessions of this activity over time will help build concentration. Don't try to finish the collage in one session. When your child is busy doing something else (or sleeping), prepare some things to add to the collage by cutting out a few small pictures or finding something that supports a current interest of his, such as animals, tractors, or trains. Put these in a bowl near the collage and add a glue stick.

Get the Big Picture
make a really big picture

WHAT YOU NEED:

- newspaper, wallpaper, or a roll of drawing paper
- a big piece of cardboard
- masking tape or sticky tape, child safety scissors, glue sticks
- stickers, magazines, junk mail, old greeting cards, gift wrap

Ready for more?

Add glitter, sequins, gift ribbon, scraps of fabric and lace, family photos, clip art, or even tiny toys–a collage can contain anything!

What is your child learning?

Completing this activity over time helps your child to learn the importance and reward of a longer-term project.

WHAT TO DO:

This is a longer activity, so be prepared to have it around for several days or even weeks!

1. Cover the big piece of cardboard entirely with paper, wrapping the paper over the edges and sticking it securely on the back with tape.
2. Find a place to put the cardboard—prop it against a wall, stick it to a door, or put it on a table.
3. Now, collect all the things you need to make a picture collage—see What You Need.
4. Talk about the "Big Picture" and what your child would like to do. Remember, the collage won't be a traditional picture of one thing; instead, it will be a collection of smaller pictures, patterns, and textures covering the whole sheet.
5. Cut or tear out any pictures that catch your eye and stick them on. If you put the cardboard on the floor or a table, your child can work from any side.
6. When your child has had enough, prop the picture up and have a look. Put the picture somewhere safe, but make sure your child can see it and continue to add new pictures and objects over time.

Another idea: Make a family photo collage with photos of family, friends, favorite toys, holidays, and special occasions.

What is your child learning?

Children learn just as well from simple games that use everyday objects. This game helps your child track a moving object in space, teaching her to use her hands and eyes in a coordinated way.

DID YOU KNOW?

Watching things move in the air switches on brain cells in both sides of the brain.

HELPFUL HINTS

Throwing and catching is very good eye-hand practice. If your child finds catching difficult, try some rolling games with soft balls that are easy to catch. Older children could have fun with a Koosh ball, which has rubber filaments all over it and is easier to catch than a smooth ball.

Falling Feathers
clap and catch

WHAT YOU NEED:

- craft feathers (get these from a craft shop or online)
- chiffon scarves (thrift stores are good places to find these)

Ready for more?

Make some small balls from rolled socks, and use these for catching and throwing—or throw them into a wastepaper basket or bucket. When you are helping your child wash her hands or helping her take a bath, drop wet washcloths and sponges for her to catch.

WHAT TO DO:

1. Sit with your child, and tell her you are going to play a catching game.
2. Put the basket of objects nearby, but not where it will distract your child.
3. Take a small chiffon scarf from the basket and hold it high above your child's hands. Say, "Ready, set, GO!" and drop the scarf for her to catch.
4. Do this several times so she gets used to catching the scarf.
5. Now take a small feather from the basket, and gently stroke your child's hands or cheek.
6. Hold the feather up high above your child's hands and say, "Ready, set, GO!" before dropping the feather for her to catch. This is harder than catching the scarf, so use smaller, curly feathers that will fall more slowly than bigger ones.
7. Keep dropping feathers and scarves for her to catch, reminding her to watch the object as it falls.

Another idea: Blow some bubbles for your child to catch with both hands. Blow them up above her, so she has time to watch and catch.

Wet and Dry
sand play

DID YOU KNOW?
Being in water reminds our brains and bodies of being in the womb.

WHAT YOU NEED:

- some play sand
- a large bowl or a big plant saucer
- small sieves, funnels, plastic bottles, corks, yogurt containers, and spoons
- a water jug

Ready for more?

Encourage your child to play in a bowl in the sink. Give him some warm, bubbly water, and add some plastic spoons, small pots and pans, yogurt containers, and so on for him to play with.

WHAT TO DO:

1. Sit with your child, and let him watch as you pour dry sand into one of the trays or bowls.
2. Play with him, using the sand toys and containers. Look at the sand, and observe how it pours and moves.
3. Take the toys out of the sand, and put some water in a plastic jug. Let your child add this to the dry sand a little at a time. Watch what happens.
4. Try not to interfere with your child's exploration of the wet sand. He may want to put lots of water in, or just a tiny bit.
5. When the sand is damp, offer your child some containers or sand molds to make castles and shapes.

Another idea: Add some toy animals or cars to the damp sand tray. Help your child to make mountains, fields, or a zoo.

HELPFUL HINTS

Most children love sand and water play. If your child does not, just play with dry sand to start with, offering small amounts in a little plastic bowl. For some young children, the aim seems to be to get as much sand as possible out of the container and onto the floor! Make sweeping up part of the game.

What is your child learning?

Feeling different textures and changing things by adding water are ways that all children learn about the world.

What is your child learning?

Making toys from simple objects is a useful lesson for children and families. Successful learning often comes from using familiar objects in new ways.

Bouncing Balls
fun with elastic

DID YOU KNOW?
Watching a bouncing object will strengthen your child's eye muscles.

WHAT YOU NEED:

- rubber bands
- some long pieces of thin elastic, around 18"
- newspaper, old wrapping paper or paper towels

Ready for more?

Tie elastic onto stuffed animals and take them for a bouncy walk. Be attentive when your child is outdoors: she will be concentrating on the ball and may not be as aware of other things.

WHAT TO DO:

1. Help your child scrunch a piece of newspaper or old wrapping paper into a ball about as big as your fist. Press it hard to make it as solid as possible.
2. Fix the ball together with elastic bands, so it is a good shape, firm enough to bounce. Try bouncing it on the floor.
3. Now tie a piece of elastic around the ball to make a bouncing toy.
4. Play bouncing games with the ball, up and down the stairs, around the room, in the garden, or on a walk to the park.
5. Make a new ball when your old one wears out.

Another idea: Make a waterproof ball by putting the paper ball in a plastic bag before fixing it with elastic bands. Now you can play in the rain or even in the bath!

Up and Down Stairs
climbing and looking

WHAT YOU NEED:

- the stairs in your home or some safe steps in a park

WHAT TO DO:

1. Stand at the bottom of the stairs with your child, holding his hand.
2. Start to climb the stairs one at a time, at your child's pace.
3. As you climb the stairs, say or sing, "Up the stairs and up the stairs and up the stairs we go. Up we go and up we go and up we go again."
4. Keep singing as you climb to the top.
5. Now look at what you can see from the top of the stairs and talk with your child about each thing. "What can we see from the top of the stairs? I can see your bed!" or "I can see the stores." If you are in the park, find a place to sit and watch the people going by. If you are at home, sit on the top step, looking down to see what you can see.
6. Go down the stairs, saying or singing, "Down the stairs and down the stairs and down the stairs we go. Down we go and down we go and down we go again."
7. If your child wants to up again, do it. If not, sit on the bottom step and see what you can see.

Another idea: Practice counting as you climb the stairs. Don't worry if your child can't count accurately yet. Listening to you count will help him a lot.

Ready for more?

Sing the same song as you go up an escalator. This is sometimes easier for your child because he won't have to concentrate on stepping and looking at the same time. Take a teddy bear up the stairs, counting as you climb, and saying, "One step, Teddy, two steps, Teddy, Three steps, Teddy." Count up to five, and then start counting again.

What is your child learning?

Watch your child to see how he climbs. An early stage is to lift one foot up (or down) a step, then bring the other foot up (or down) to join it. This is quite normal, and some children walk downstairs in this way for a long time.

HELPFUL HINTS

If your child is still learning about stairs, stand behind him and put your hands under his arms to help him. Find steps and low walls in your favorite places, such as the park, and practice singing simple songs and counting as you walk.

The Hat Dance
a stopping and starting game

WHAT YOU NEED:

- a collection of hats—helmets, sunhats, caps, toboggans (make sure at least one of the hats fits you)
- a full-length mirror so the children can see themselves
- some music on an MP3 player or CD player

Ready for more?

Play the hat game again, but this time, take another hat every time the music stops. How many hats can you balance on your head? Play some more stopping and starting games. How many blocks can you put in a bucket before the music stops? How many pens can you put in a cup?

WHAT TO DO:

1. Spread all the hats out on the floor and walk among them with your child, looking at the different hats.
2. Turn on the music and walk or dance around the hats. When the music stops, choose a hat each, put it on.
3. Turn the music on and dance around the remaining hats.
4. When the music stops, take off the hat and put it back on the floor.
5. Play again, but choose a different hat and do a different dance.
6. Continue as long as your child is enjoying the game.
7. When you have finished, toss all the hats back into a basket or box.

Another idea: Put a pair of gloves by each hat. When the music stops, you must put on the hat and the gloves.

HELPFUL HINTS

Some children get so involved in dancing that they don't hear the music stop. Make sure you wait until your child has really stopped. Get some plastic plates and wooden spoons, or some pots and metal spoons, and have a marching band. Using your whole body helps with a sense of rhythm.

DID YOU KNOW?

Stopping needs lots of practice. Your child's brain needs more time to stop than an adult's does.

What is your child learning?

Moving confidently is a skill every child can learn. Give your child lots of opportunities to move rhythmically to music.

Spongy Feet
squishy feelings

WHAT YOU NEED:

- a flat space outside and a warm day
- a big piece of foam sheet (a camping mattress is ideal)
- silver duct tape (from bargain shops or DIY stores)
- baby bubble bath mixed with a little water
- a towel

WHAT TO DO:

1. Put the foam sheet on a smooth surface outside, and tape it down securely. Now, pour some bubble bath and water mixture on the sheet. Not too much!
2. Take your shoes and socks off, and roll up your trousers. Help your child do the same. Put the towel nearby, but not too close.
3. Now, hold hands with your child and step onto the foam. Start to move around. Your feet will make bubbles come out of the foam.
4. Keep walking and stomping so you make a layer of bubbles on the foam!
5. When you have had enough, step carefully off the edge of the foam mat and dry your feet on the towel.

Ready for more?
Fix sponges on your feet by pulling socks over them. Step in bubbly water, and then walk on a dry sidewalk or patio to make bubbly footprints.

Another idea: Try the same game with a big sheet of bubble wrap, securely taped down.

HELPFUL HINTS

If your child is less steady on his feet, hold both of his hands. This will give him more confidence. This activity makes some children very excited. Use a low, calm voice, and keep the activity short. Help him calm down afterward by wrapping him in a big warm towel and singing a quiet song.

What is your child learning?

Balance is an essential skill for all physical activity. This is a good way to practice. Your child is also learning to try new experiences, which will link more cells in his brain.

What is your child learning?

Your child is learning to link objects with their uses. This is an important part of organizing her world.

I Wonder
collections in a sensory bag

WHAT YOU NEED:

- a fabric bag, such as a shoe bag or a pillowcase
- some themed items, such as: bathroom things—a comb, toothbrush, toothpaste, and washcloth; food; or clothes

Ready for more?

Play the sensory game with toys. Start with just one toy in the bag. See if your child can name it, and ask her for a color if she is beginning to know her colors.

WHAT TO DO:

1. Start the activity with the objects on the floor next to the bag.
2. Sit with your child and look at all the objects, naming them and talking about how they are used.
3. Put the objects in the bag and let your child feel in the bag; see if she can name the object before she pulls it out. Say, "Can you feel it? What is it? Now, 1-2-3; let's look!"
4. Take a turn yourself and see what you can find. Exaggerate the "1-2-3; let's look!" so your child is anticipating and listening to you.
5. See if your child can guess the hidden object if you say, "I can feel something that you use to clean your teeth. Can you guess what I can feel?"
6. Continue playing until your child has had enough. Then let her help you put the things away.

DID YOU KNOW?

Using the sense of touch makes learning links in the brain stronger and more permanent.

What is your child learning?

Your child is learning that taking turns can be fun. This will reinforce the pleasure your child takes in playing with others.

My Turn, Your Turn
a turn-taking game

WHAT YOU NEED:

- stacking bricks in a basket or box

Ready for more?

Start the tower, and then ask each other for a particular brick: "Now can you put a red brick on the tower?" and, "Which color shall I put next?" Play "Thank you" with the bricks: "Can you give me a blue brick? Thank you! Can you give me a red brick?" Use a stuffed animal to help: "Can you give Teddy a brown brick? Thank you."

WHAT TO DO:

1. Sit on the floor with your child. You will need a flat surface for brick building, so avoid carpets or rugs.
2. Take one brick out of the basket and put it on the floor.
3. Say, "Your turn," and encourage your child to put a brick on top of yours.
4. Continue to take turns building the bricks until the tower falls down. Make this enjoyable by saying, "Here it goes—crash, bang, all fall down."
5. Now ask, "Again?" and build the tower again together. Most children will play this game again and again.
6. When your child is tired (or when you are!), take turns to toss the bricks back in the basket one at a time.

Another idea: Build towers with cans or cartons from your kitchen cupboard. These may make wobbly towers, which are even more fun.

Who Am I?
simple dressing up with a mirror

WHAT YOU NEED:

- a shatterproof mirror at child height
- plastic sunglasses or empty glasses frames
- simple dress-up items—scarves, hats, jewelry, shoes, handbags
- face paints if you have them

Ready for more?

Add some cloaks and masks for superhero play, or some fairy-tale clothes to play storytelling. Children love grown-up clothes such as high-heeled shoes, ties, and jackets. Take some photos of yourselves in the mirror, and print them or send them to friends and relatives.

WHAT TO DO:

1. If there is a long mirror in your hall, your own bedroom, or your child's room, you could play the game there.
2. Put the dress-up items on the floor and sit or kneel by your child, so you can both see both of you.
3. Try on some of the dress-up clothes together, talking about how you look in them. Ask your child's opinion—"Do you like this hat or this one?" or "Do you think I look like Daddy in these glasses?"
4. Encourage your child to pretend to be other people as she tries on the clothes.
5. Sing a song or do some funny walking as you look at yourselves in the mirror.
6. If you have similar objects, follow your child and dress up just like her. This will cause a lot of amusement.

Another idea: Make some face paints from moisturizer with food coloring added. Put them in little containers for your child to use, and make a little "dressing table" from a box or small table, adding combs, brushes, and hand mirrors.

HELPFUL HINTS

Some children find buttons and other fastenings difficult. Dressing up is a great way to practice. Looking at her own face in a mirror helps your child recognize her own features and learn how others see her. She will begin to understand herself as a separate being.

What is your child learning?

Pretending to be someone else teaches your child about feelings and the way other people act. This helps her develop social skills and empathy.

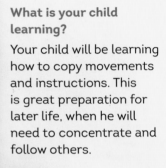

What is your child learning?

Your child will be learning how to copy movements and instructions. This is great preparation for later life, when he will need to concentrate and follow others.

Touch Your Nose
learning body parts

WHAT YOU NEED:

- No special equipment needed for this activity.

Ready for more?

Play the same game standing up. As your child gets used to this game, give him instructions without doing the action yourself. See if he can follow your words, but don't go too fast, and give him clues if he is finding it difficult. Make the game even more complicated by asking him to do two different things—"Put one hand on your head and one hand on your tummy," or "Put your finger on your tummy and your foot in the air."

WHAT TO DO:

1. Sit opposite your child on the floor or the couch.
2. Tell him you are going to play a game called Put Your Finger on Your Nose. Explain that you will tell him what to do, and encourage him to copy you.
3. Now put your finger on your own nose, saying, "Put your finger on your nose." Ask your child to copy you, and praise him when he does.
4. Continue playing the game, saying the instruction and doing it yourself. Use movements and words such as, "Put your finger on your hair" or "Put your hand on your head."
5. If he wants to continue, try with two hands: "Put your two hands on your cheeks." Continue with your feet, your neck, and so on.

Another idea: Play the game with a doll or stuffed animal.

HELPFUL HINTS

Sit closer if he is having difficulty copying you, or help him by holding his hand. Match the game with the body parts your child knows—eyebrows, eyelashes, ankles, and thighs may be too difficult at first.

After You!
taking turns and sharing

WHAT YOU NEED:

- a child's tea set or some plastic picnic plates, cups, jug, utensils, and so on
- some pretend or real food
- milk, juice, or water
- a small table and a cushion each

Ready for more?

Have picnics on the grass or even indoors on wet days, but concentrate on good manners and polite behavior. Model the behavior you want your child to learn.

WHAT TO DO:

1. Help your child set the table for your tea party, talking about how many plates, cups, and utensils you need.
2. Sit on a cushion each and begin your tea party. Concentrate on sharing and being polite.
3. Pour drinks and pass around the food together, remembering to ask what the other person would like. Make sure to discuss what you are doing.
4. Model good behavior by saying *please* and *thank you,* along with questions such as, "Could you pass the tea?" or "Would you like a cookie?"
5. When your child copies you, praise her behavior by saying, "That was really polite," or "You shared those really well."

HELPFUL HINTS

Some children may need help with pouring and serving. Little china milk jugs are easier to use and more stable to pick up and put down. Setting a place for each person takes practice. Try first with a stuffed animal on each chair around your dining table to make things easier.

What is your child learning?

Your child is learning that mealtimes are special occasions and that the conventions of meals and manners are important and valuable skills to learn. She will also learn hand control from serving, pouring, and cutting food.

Sticker Fun
following instructions

WHAT YOU NEED:

- some sheets of stickers or stars (get these from stationery shops or toys shops)
- camera or phone with a camera

WHAT TO DO:

1. Look at the stickers together, and talk about them if they have pictures on them.
2. Explain to your child that you are going to ask him to put the stickers in funny places on his body!
3. Hand him the first sticker and say, "Can you put this sticker on your leg?"
4. When he has done that, continue the game by asking him to put stickers on other parts of his body or clothes.
5. Praise him each time he gets it right.
6. When he has had enough, or you run out of stickers, take a photo of your child before the stickers start to fall off!

Another idea: Put the stickers on a teddy bear or a favorite toy.

DID YOU KNOW?

Blowing bubbles helps children's breathing, and this helps with talking.

HELPFUL HINTS

Hold your child's hand in yours to help her blow bubbles. Younger or less mature children may like to pat bubbles on a tray or other flat surface.

Bubble and Blow
fun with bubbles

WHAT YOU NEED:

- some bubbles and bubble wands
- straws
- scissors
- small plastic bowls
- an old towel for drips and spills

WHAT TO DO:

This is a good activity to do in the garden or the park.

1. Play with the bubbles and blowers, holding the blower for your child if she finds it difficult.
2. Watch the bubbles as they float, and talk about the colors, shapes, and sizes. Catch them and pop them.
3. Blow some bubbles near your child so she can reach or chase them.
4. Now cut a small nick about 1 inch from the top of a straw. Some children get mixed up between blowing and sucking, and this will stop them swallowing the bubble mixture!
5. Put some bubble mixture in a small bowl, and show your child how to blow gently into this mixture to produce a pile of bubbles.

Another idea: Mix some bubble mixture with food coloring. Make bubble prints by blowing into a bowl of bubbles and putting a sheet of paper over the top to make a print.

What is your child learning?

Getting involved in simple activities like blowing bubbles, helps children in realizing that they can do things for themselves. This will help your child's confidence.

Ready for more?

Find a small battery-powered fan. Use this to blow the bubbles around indoors and outside. Use coat hangers or bendy twigs to make giant bubbles in a bowl of bubbly water.

Noodle Heads
playing with textures

WHAT YOU NEED:

- a pack of instant ramen noodles
- a big plastic bowl
- cooking oil
- small plastic plates
- glitter or sequins

WHAT TO DO:

1. Cook the noodles by pouring boiling water over them in a bowl. Drain them thoroughly and let them cool.
2. Now help your child mix the noodles with half a teaspoon of cooking oil to keep them from sticking together.
3. Work together to spoon the noodles onto some plates, and sit with your child to play with them.
4. Practice picking up just one noodle between your finger and thumb. Take the noodle to an empty plate and gently put it down. Use spoons and forks to lift and share the noodles. Sprinkle sequins or glitter on top to make "dinner" for each other.
5. Have a noodle party with some stuffed animals.
6. When you have finished playing, put the noodles in the garden for the birds to eat.

DID YOU KNOW?

Careful movements with finger and thumb are essential for writing.

Ready for more?

Cut the big sides from cereal boxes, and save these for painting and tactile experiences like this. Make patterns on these cards; the starch in the noodles will stick them without glue. Picking up small objects, such as dried peas or small buttons, and putting these in a tin will challenge your child's concentration and dexterity.

What is your child learning?

Using hands and fingers with tactile materials teaches your child to manage slippery stuff. It also helps him concentrate by offering him interesting and unusual materials to work with.

HELPFUL HINTS

Using tweezers is another way of keeping your child involved as he learns to manage fingers and hands. Get some plastic ones suitable for children.

What is your child learning?

By exercising hand and finger control in enjoyable activities, your child is learning essential skills for learning to write, draw, and use all sorts of tools.

Poking, Poking
finger play with dough

DID YOU KNOW?

Pointing is a good thing to practice. It is a first step in holding tools, such as pencils.

WHAT YOU NEED:

- a rolling pin
- a flat surface for rolling out the dough
- to make some simple dough:
  - 4 cups of flour
  - 2 cups of table salt
  - 2 cups of warm water
  - a wooden spoon
  - a bowl

Ready for more?

Roll some of the dough into "sausages" and let your child cut these into pieces with children's scissors.

WHAT TO DO:

1. Help your child measure and mix the dough. Put the salt and flour in the bowl and mix thoroughly.
2. Now add the warm water a bit at a time, mixing between each addition.
3. When the mixture makes a soft dough, tip it out of the bowl and let your child play with it without any intervention from you.
4. Help her roll out some of the dough into a flat cake and play a poking game, using your first finger on each hand to make finger pokes all over the dough.
5. Gather the dough up again, roll it out and play again, seeing who can make the most pokes in the dough.
6. When you have finished, put the dough in an airtight plastic bag in the fridge—it will keep for several days.

What is your child learning?

In this game, your child will be learning about shapes and sizes by matching them against his own body. Looking at baby clothes will help him understand about growth.

Giant Feet!
getting an idea of size

WHAT YOU NEED:

- a full-length mirror at child height (in the hall or a bedroom)
- very big clothing such as adult gloves, hats and socks, rainboots, big flip-flops, men's shoes, slippers
- very small clothing, such as baby shoes and socks, little pajamas, baby mittens

Ready for more?

Take some photos of the clothing and shoes. Make these photos into a memory game where you match the big and small pairs.

WHAT TO DO:

1. Collect all the clothes and mix them up in a laundry basket. Sit with your child near the mirror.
2. Help him take the clothes out of the basket, talking about them and who could wear them. Try to use two-word descriptions, such as *big boots* or *baby socks*.
3. Try some of the clothes and shoes on. Look at yourselves in the mirror.
4. Ask him if he thinks any of the clothes fit him, or if they would fit you. Put on some of the biggest things yourself and say, "Too big!" Put your feet next to the baby shoes and say, "Too small!"
5. Sort the clothes into a pile of big ones and a pile of small ones. Now put them all back in the basket.

Another idea: Use the collection of clothes to have a family dress-up race. Make it harder for the adults by giving each adult a doll or teddy bear to dress in the baby clothes, as well as dressing themselves. Take some photos.

Sort It Out
sorting natural objects

WHAT YOU NEED:

- baskets or boxes for sorting
- a big, shallow basket or box
- a collection of natural materials, such as shells, stones, cones, twigs, and leaves

Ready for more?

Collect or buy some natural objects, such as shells, cones, polished stones, plants, or driftwood. These will all give a sense of calm to your home. When you collect objects on walks, take pictures of the places you went, so you can make a photo book to go with your collection of memories.

WHAT TO DO:

1. Put a collection of natural objects in a big box or basket.
2. Arrange some smaller containers (baskets, boxes, or bowls) near the collection.
3. Begin to look at the objects you have collected. Remind your child of the place and time when you collected the object. Talk about what it was like, the weather, and what you were doing.
4. Now, look closely at the object. Talk about the texture, color, and pattern. Feel the surface against your hands or even your cheek. What does the object smell like?
5. Now look at another of the objects. Try to choose something that looks or feels different.
6. After you have looked at some of the objects, begin to sort them into baskets.

Another idea: Make sure your child has some toys made from natural materials, such as wood, and encourage her to collect natural objects on walks and visits.

HELPFUL HINTS

Use a small collection—around four or five objects—while your child develops her language skills.

What is your child learning?

Your child is learning that natural objects have as much interest as store-bought toys.

Who Is That?
recognizing faces

WHAT YOU NEED:

- some photos of family members in different places, clothes, and seasons

Ready for more?

Help your child tear or cut photos of faces from magazines, and together, make a scrapbook of faces.

WHAT TO DO:

This simple activity should be a frequent part of your child's life, celebrating and remembering family occasions and people he knows. Framed photos of family members and friends make a real contribution to your child's life. Make sure there are plenty of these in your home.

1. The photos can be printed on paper, in an album, viewed on a computer, or viewed on a mobile phone. (Make sure your phone has a big enough screen for the child to see the faces.)
2. Make sure your collection contains some photos of grandparents, family friends, children, and your child, too!
3. Sit with your child in a comfortable chair as you look at the photos.
4. Ask him if he can name the person or people in each photo. Remind him of the occasion and place where the photo was taken.

Another idea: Make photo books of holidays and special occasions and have these handy to look at when you have a few minutes spare.

HELPFUL HINTS

Recognizing themselves in photos is difficult for some children. Take your time, and play plenty of photo games. Take photos of your child regularly and show him the photos as soon after taking them as you can. Digital cameras and mobile phones are great for this!

What is your child learning?

Your child is learning a sense of self and of community, the key people in his life, and how to recognize himself. This will help him feel more secure and safe.

The big space is daunting for some children—which is why staying with them is so important: you can give them support and confidence. If your child finds the tools difficult to use, let her play with the paint in her hands.

Splatters and Dots
early painting

WHAT YOU NEED:

- children's paint
- paint sponges
- big paintbrushes
- big pieces of paper (newspaper or the back of wallpaper will do)
- masking tape
- aprons

Ready for more?

Ask a friend with a young child to come for a painting morning, and join your children for a group painting session in your backyard. Use the sponges and brushes with a bucket of water to paint the sidewalk, fence, or back door.

What is your child learning?

Your child is learning to work on a big scale, to use tools, and to persevere with a big project. She may need your help and encouragement to stay focused.

WHAT TO DO:

1. Help your child stick a big piece of paper to a low table to make a really big painting surface.

2. Put some paint in plastic mugs or small, empty water bottles. If you cut the tops off these and put them back upside down, the tops will fit in the bottoms of the bottles to make non-spill paint pots. These bottles also slow down the drying out of paint!

3. Put your aprons on, put the paints where your child can reach them, and offer the paintbrushes and sponges.

4. Suggest that your child can stand up to paint if she likes.

5. Stay with your child as she paints, and join in if she invites you (but don't take over, and don't try to make it a picture!). The idea is to explore the paint and applicators, not to paint a picture.

6. When the painting is finished and dry, find a space to pin it up so everyone can see your child's work.

Another idea: Leave the painting activity out all day so your child can return to it more than once.

Up in the Air
tossing your teddy bear in a blanket

WHAT YOU NEED:

- a teddy bear or other favorite stuffed animal
- a piece of fabric about 1 square yard (stretchy, fleece, or knitted fabric is best)
- a space to move around in

Ready for more?

Try the same game with a balloon. This is more difficult to do, as the balloon is lighter and more likely to fall off the edge of the fabric.

WHAT TO DO:

1. Explain to your child that you are going to play a game with his teddy bear (or another favorite toy). Show him the fabric or blanket, and practice holding a corner in each hand so you can lift and bounce together.
2. Put the fabric on the floor, and put the teddy bear in the middle.
3. Carefully pick up two corners each and gently lift teddy into the air.
4. Begin to bounce the teddy bear so he moves up and down on the blanket. Say, "Teddy Bear is bouncing, bouncing, bouncing; Teddy Bear is bouncing in the air."
5. Now, bounce a bit harder so the teddy bear goes further up into the air. Say, "Higher, higher, up and down, Teddy Bear's bouncing up and down."
6. Now gently lower the blanket and give the bear a hug together.

HELPFUL HINTS

Some children need help to hold on with both hands. If your child's grip is weak, do not bounce too hard, or he will lose his hold. Some children get overexcited, so you need to play the game very gently and use a quiet tone of voice.

What is your child learning?

This game is about trust and working together. Your child will be learning how to control his actions so the game works for his teddy bear.

What is your child learning?

Your child is learning about being safe while exploring the concept of being lost. Talking about these feelings is very important for your child's development.

Lost!
caring for a lost toy

DID YOU KNOW?

Imagining and empathizing are higher-order thinking skills.

WHAT YOU NEED:

- a stuffed animal that your child doesn't know
- a luggage label or some card and string
- scissors (for adult use only)

Ready for more?

Make up a story about the lost toy, inventing some of the things it has done, where it came from, and even who it belonged to.

WHAT TO DO:

This game needs you to keep a secret!

1. Write a message on the label. It can say anything you like, but it should go something like this: "I am lost and cold and hungry. Please look after me." Tie the message around the neck of the stuffed animal.

2. Hide the toy where your child will find it the following day, such as sitting on the back porch. Let your child find the toy, and read the label to her.

3. Talk with your child about being lost, and ask her what you should do with the toy. Accept her suggestions; she may want to give the toy a name, give it some food, make a bed for it, or put up a notice to find its owner. Try to respond positively to what she says.

4. When your child has lost interest in the toy, you have a decision. You could remove the toy and leave a note from its owner who has come to fetch it; or, you could say that no one is coming, so the toy should live with you permanently.

Jelly on the Plate
play with familiar substances

WHAT YOU NEED:

- some small plastic plates
- a packet of gelatin
- hot water
- two plastic bowls
- spoons, forks, a whisk

WHAT TO DO:

1. Make the gelatin in advance and put it somewhere cool to set.
2. Sit at a table or worktop with your child.
3. Spoon some gelatin onto a plastic plate for each of you.
4. Explore the gelatin with fingers, hands, spoons, and forks. Encourage your child to really get involved in feeling the gelatin, squeezing it between his fingers and fists, patting it, and pushing it around the plate.
5. Now let your child help you to whisk some of the gelatin in another bowl. Explore the gelatin with your hands and fingers.

Another idea: Put some objects in the gelatin before it sets—pieces of paper, polystyrene, beads, marbles, or even small toys, and let your child find them.

Ready for more?

Have some finger fun with pudding or yogurt on a small tray, drawing and making marks with fingers and hands. Freeze some very small items in ice cubes, put the ice cubes in a bowl of water, and play with them as they melt and release the objects.

HELPFUL HINTS

If your child has any skin allergies, let him experience these activities in gloves. Some children don't like playing with these tactile materials. Slightly warming some pudding or yogurt sometimes makes a difference to how they feel. Or try putting them in plastic zip-lock bags. Close the bags and play with the materials from the outside.

What is your child learning?

Your child is learning about textures and the behavior of solids and liquids. This play will be essential for your child's early science learning.

DID YOU KNOW?

Playing with these materials is a vital part of strengthening your child's hands.

Inside!
make a den

WHAT YOU NEED:

- a cardboard box, big enough for your child to fit in
- a blanket, some cushions
- a stuffed animal or two
- a thin scarf or a piece of net curtain
- tape
- a CD player with some quiet music

WHAT TO DO:

1. Put the box on its side, and invite your child to climb inside the "house." If you can get a really big box, you could get in, too!
2. If you can't, sit or lie down next to the box house so you can talk to your child.
3. Ask her if she would like some things to make her house a home. Offer cushions, a blanket, or a stuffed animal or teddy bear.
4. Suggest that some music would be nice, and get a music player if she wants one.
5. Ask your child if she would like a door on her house. If she does, tape a piece of very thin fabric across the top of the opening to make a door.
6. Most children love being inside boxes, so if your child likes her house, ask her if she might like a snack and a drink inside of it. Sit outside the house to have a snack, too, and talk to her through the curtain.

Another idea: Use empty cartons for boats, buses, and trains. They are free, with good play value, and they are recyclable—the best sort of toy!

Ready for more?

Get into the habit of using boxes and cartons. Make one into a house for a teddy bear or doll, with a bed and table inside of it. Join some boxes together with tape in a line to make a train with cars. Fill the cars with toys. Let your child "drive" the train from the first box.

What is your child learning?

Being in her own space helps your child feel secure and in control. She will also be learning about being quiet and reflective. Quiet activities release calming chemicals in the body and brain. These help your child learn.

Stretchy, Scrunchy
fun with wrists and ankles

WHAT YOU NEED:

- some bracelets or hair scrunchies
- lengths of ribbon or strips of interesting fabric
- a basket
- some music on tape, CD, or radio

Ready for more?

Dance outside to your own songs or a portable player or radio.

What is your child learning?

A sense of rhythm and a love for dance and music are both good things for children to learn, and the younger they learn them, the better!

WHAT TO DO:

1. Show the ribbons and scrunchies to your child and help him put some on his wrists, arms, and ankles.
2. Experiment with different dancing steps, swirling, twisting, waving, and jumping.
3. Now put some music on—something quiet would be good. Dance with your child, holding his hands and following his steps, dancing together and by yourself.
4. Ask your child if he would like to do a dance for you to watch. If he does, be appreciative of his effort and give him praise.
5. Try to dance all around the house together.

Another idea: Find or buy some bells, and add these to the bangles and scrunchies for dances.

DID YOU KNOW?

Music and dancing will help your child to learn. Rhythm helps memory.

HELPFUL HINTS

Dancing is a talent that some children have and some don't. Encourage all of your child's efforts, however uncoordinated he might be. He will get better with practice! Some boys (and girls) think dancing is "girly." Remind your child of the strong male dance roles they see on television and in movies. Make sure you play more upbeat music sometimes, and offer your child a good range of colors to wear.

Index